June 2017
Cosford Air Museum

To my gorgeou

Love you (& weren't the homemade ice-creams AMAZING!)

Mum

♡ ♡

X X X X

Picture credits:
t=top b=bottom m=middle l=left r=right c=centre

6t: Tech. Sgt. Cecilio Ricardo, 15t, 14b, 28t: U.S. Air Force photo,
30t: Tech. Sgt. Keith Brown, 7b: Darren Murphy,
8-9t: Ronny Bar, 8b,9b, 19, 24-25t:Bettmann/CORBIS,
11m: Pedro Soares, 14-15c: Alan Wesley, 17t: Ian Robertson,
18t: Den Pascoe, 20, 27, 29, 30b, 31, 32t, 33, 34m, 34b, 35, 38t, 41t,: DOD, DVIC, 21b: Corbis,
22-23b, 40-41m: Jim Ross, 24b, 42t, 43m: U.S. Airforce Photo,
25b: Sergey Riabsev, 32b: Yevgeny Khaldei/CORBIS,
34t: Ian Robertson, 36t: Spc. Russell J. Good,
36m: Spc. Cory Montgomery, U.S. Army,
38-39b: Menso van Westrhenen, 43t: Graham Bloomfield.

Published By: Robert Frederick Ltd.
4 North Parade, Bath, England.

First Published: 2006

Printed in China.

COMBAT AIRCRAFT

Contents

Know Your Combat Aircraft

Combat aircraft are aeroplanes used by the military during war. Aeroplanes came to be used for military purposes within a few years of the first flight of a heavier-than-air aircraft in 1903. Hot air balloons and zeppelins were used before this to gather information about enemy troops.

Types of combat aircraft

Combat aircraft can be broadly divided into fighter, bomber, tanker, trainer, surveillance and transport aircraft. Fighters and bombers carry weapons and are directly involved in combat missions. Fighter planes are designed mainly to fight other aircraft. They are small, fast and easy to manoeuvre. Bombers are used to drop bombs on targets on the ground, such as buildings and bridges.

The B-2 Spirit is a multi-role stealth bomber that is not easily detected by enemy radars. It is the most expensive aircraft ever built

SR-71

Type:	strategic reconnaissance aircraft
Manufactured by:	Lockheed Martin, U.S.A.
Crew:	One or two
Maximum speed:	3,529.56 km/h (2,193.17 mph)

Unarmed combat aircraft

Apart from fighters and bombers, air forces of the world also employ other types of aircraft that do not carry weapons. Some, like tankers, carry fuel to other attack aircraft, while others, such as transport aircraft, carry troops and equipment from one place to another. Surveillance or reconnaissance aircraft fly over the enemy targets and take pictures of their troops and facilities. Lastly,there are trainer aircraft, which are used to train pilots.

The SR-71 was an American reconnaissance aircraft that was in service from 1964 to 1998. This aircraft was one of the fastest of its type and not even one SR-71 has ever been shot down

MiG-25

Type:	reconnaissance aircraft with limited, accurate bombing capability
Manufactured by:	Mikoyan-Gurevich, Russia
Crew:	Single
Maximum speed:	3,000 km/h (1,864 mph)
Weapons:	4-6 missiles

B-2 Spirit

Type:	two/three-seat strategic 'stealth' bomber and missile-launch platform
Manufactured by:	Northrop Grumman, U.S.A.
Crew:	Two
Maximum speed:	1,000 km/h (621.37 mph)
Weapons:	18,144 kg (40,000 lb) of bombs; 16 nuclear

Combat helicopters

Helicopters are also an important part of any defence force. Like fixed wing aircraft, combat helicopters are also of various kinds. Attack helicopters carry machine guns and missiles to fight enemy troops. Some attack helicopters are equipped with air-to-air missiles for defensive purposes. Attack helicopters are mainly used to provide air support for ground troops. Transport helicopters are used to move men and machinery. Helicopters can also be used to drop supplies and paratroopers, and carry out search and rescue missions. Since helicopters can take-off and land from just about anywhere, they are often preferred to fixed wing aircraft in war zones.

The Sikorsky S-70 is one of the most widely used combat helicopters. It is in service in the armed forces of over 20 countries

The First Warplanes

The first warplanes were simply aircraft that flew over the enemy camp to spy on them and drop a grenade. As long as the enemy did not have any aircraft of its own, this worked well. However, when aeroplanes became popular, warplanes were armed with weapons to engage in aerial combat.

Early combat aircraft

The first instance of aerial warfare was during the French Revolution in 1794. Some French army officers flew up in a balloon to spy on the Austrian forces. Balloons began to play a vital role in observing enemy movements. They were used during the American Civil War to track the movements of the Southern Confederate forces. Inspired by this, Count Ferdinand von Zeppelin of Germany developed the zeppelin, a balloon-like aircraft that could be steered.

Italo-Turkish War

The successful flights conducted by the Wright brothers in 1903 led to balloons being replaced by fixed wing aircraft in warfare. The first successful use of these aircraft was during the Italo-Turkish War (1911-1912). Following a reconnaissance flight over Turkish military bases in Libya, on November 1, the Italians dropped the first-ever bomb from the air on the Turkish troops. This incident started a race between nations to develop military aircraft.

The Germans used zeppelins during World War I to spy on enemy troops and conduct bombing operations

The BE.2 was a reconnaissance aircraft. It was the first military aircraft used by Britain

Pre-World War aeroplanes

The build-up to World War I witnessed the production of several innovative combat aircraft, some of which became outdated even before the war. The German monoplane Rumpler Taube is one such aircraft. It was the first German military plane to be mass-produced. Being their first practical military plane, the Germans used the aircraft as a fighter, bomber, surveillance plane and trainer. However, the rapid advancement of aviation during the war made the plane obsolete by 1914.

BE.2

Type:	reconnaissance aircraft
Manufactured by:	Royal Aircraft Factory, U.K.
Crew:	Two
Maximum speed:	116 km/h (72 mph)
Weapons:	1 machine gun; 102 kg (224 lb) bomb

The Rumpler Taube was at first named Etrich Taube after its designer Igo Etrich. The aircraft was widely used by Italy, Germany and Austria-Hungary

Rumpler Taube

Type:	bomber, trainer and reconnaissance aircraft
Manufactured by:	Rumpler, Germany
Crew:	Two
Maximum speed:	100 km/h (60 mph)
Weapons:	Rifles and pistols; bombs

World War I Fighters

Fighter aircraft were first developed during World War I, starting with the aerial bombing of Turkish troops by the Italians in 1911. However, despite rapid technological advance in aviation, most of the early World War I aircraft were used for reconnaissance purposes. The first true fighter plane emerged almost a year after the war began.

A daring mission

The biggest challenge faced by the designers of early fighters was the positioning of the aircraft's guns. The ideal position for the gun was between the pilot and the nose of the aircraft, as this enabled easy firing as well as repairing, if the gun jammed. However, this was impossible as the fired bullets would strike the propeller. Roland Garros, a French pilot, overcame this problem by attaching protective metal wedges to the wooden propeller blades. Garros shot down three German planes using this improved fighter.

Fokker's design

On April 18, 1915, Garros and his fighter was shot down and captured by the Germans. The famous German aircraft designer Anthony Fokker studied the captured plane in detail. He then introduced the interrupter gear, which would allow the gun to fire between the blades of the spinning propeller. This device was fitted to the Fokker E-1 monoplanes that terrorised the Allied forces. The innovation was so successful that the period was known as the Fokker Scourge.

Fokker D.VII

Manufactured by:	Fokker Aeroplanbau, Germany
Crew:	Single
Maximum speed:	186 km/h (116 mph)
Weapons:	Two machine guns

Fighters of Allied forces

In 1916 France introduced the Nieuport 17 and Britain its first fighter, the Sopwith 1 1/2 Strutter. They were inspired by a Fokker plane that was forced to land in enemy territory due to fog. The British and the French conducted detailed studies of the captured plane and developed better combat aircraft. The Nieuport 17, a biplane fighter, had a powerful engine and large wings. In fact, it was so good that it was soon adopted by all the Allied air forces.

Roland Garros improvised his Morane-Saulnier Type L fighter by attaching metal wedges to its propellers

Morane-Saulnier Type L

Manufactured by:	Morane-Saulnier, France
Crew:	One or two
Maximum speed:	115 km/h (71 mph)
Weapons:	One machine gun

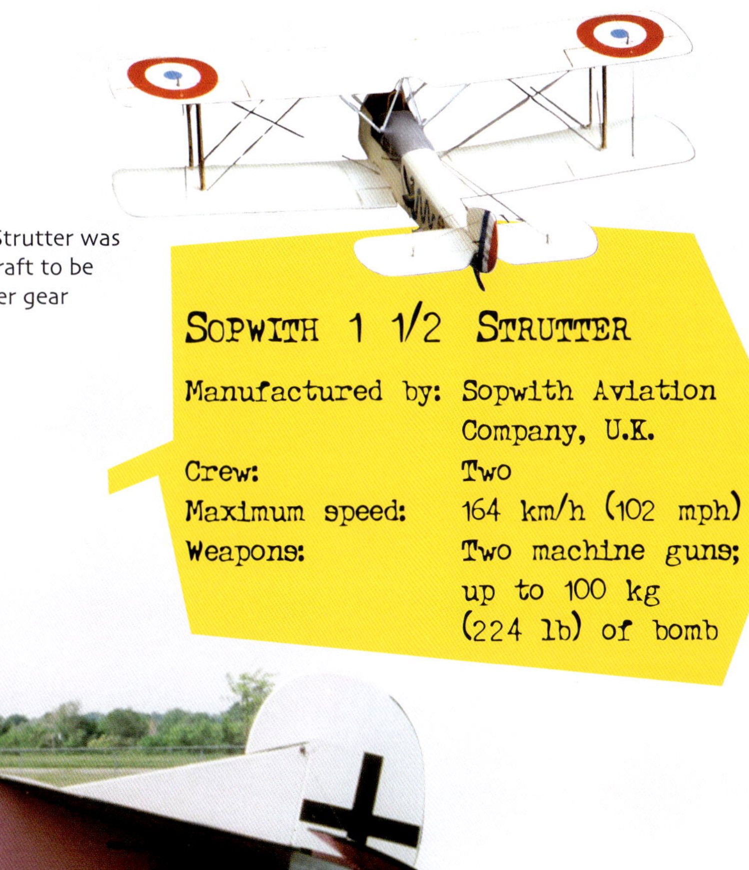

The Sopwith 1 1/2 Strutter was the first British aircraft to be built with interrupter gear

Sopwith 1 1/2 Strutter

Manufactured by:	Sopwith Aviation Company, U.K.
Crew:	Two
Maximum speed:	164 km/h (102 mph)
Weapons:	Two machine guns; up to 100 kg (224 lb) of bomb

When the Allied forces developed aircraft similar to the E-1 the Germans came up with a more advanced fighter – the Fokker D.VII. This plane was introduced in 1918 leading to a second Fokker Scourge

The Fight Intensifies

By the summer of 1916, the Allied forces, led by Britain and France, began to rule the skies. The Germans were helpless against the combined strengths of the Sopwith 1 1/2 Strutter and the Nieuport 17. They knew that they had to act quickly to regain air superiority.

Albatros D.I

During the Battle of Somme, the strong Allied air forces spread terror among the enemy by bombarding their ammunition dumps and supply systems. It was a major victory for the Allied forces. Responding swiftly, the Germans hurried the production of a revolutionary new combat plane, the Albatros D.I. Oswald Boelke, the famous German combat pilot, trained fighter pilots and formed hunting squadrons, known as Jastas. The Jastas used the new Albatros D.I to chase enemy planes down and destroy them.

Albatros D.I

Manufactured by:	Albatros Werke, Germany
Crew:	One
Maximum speed:	175 km/h (109 mph)
Weapons:	Two machine guns

Bloody April

The Jastas were most successful during the Battle of Arras in April 1917. Although the battle was being fought on their homeland, the weary French withdrew from action. The British continued the fight with over 350 aircraft. However, they were no match for the Jastas who had just 100 aircraft. The Royal Flying Corps were nearly destroyed with the loss of 240 aircraft and over 200 men during that 'Bloody April'.

Bristol F2B

Manufactured by:	Bristol Aeroplane Company, U.K.
Crew:	Two
Maximum speed:	198 km/h (123 mph)
Weapons:	Three machine guns; 108 kg (240 lb) of bomb

SOPWITH CAMEL

Manufactured by:	Sopwith Aviation Company, U.K.
Crew:	Single
Maximum speed:	185 km/h (115 mph)
Weapons:	Two machine guns

The Sopwith Camel is considered to be one of the best Allied aircraft of World War I

The Bristol Fighters were most affected during the Bloody April campaign. However, the aircraft survived its initial failure to become one of the toughest Allied fighters of the war

SOPWITH CAMEL

Following the Battle of Arras, Britain began training its pilots on the new Sopwith Camel, in a bid to regain control of the skies. By the end of 1917, the British had succeeded in their plan. The Sopwith Camel shot down well over a thousand aircraft and effectively ended German supremacy in aerial combat.

In between the World Wars

After World War I it was obvious that combat aircraft were going to play a deciding role in future wars. The years between the two World Wars were spent in developing new and improved fighters and bombers to fulfil this role. There were several innovations in combat aircraft between 1919-1938, all of which made them deadlier than ever.

A complete makeover

During World War I planes were made of wood and cloth. In the years after the war, fighters were made by fixing metal plates on to a wooden frame. The interwar period also witnessed the development of fighters that could fly faster and higher. The increased speed and height meant that cockpits had to be enclosed.

Polikarpov I-16

Designed by:	Soviet OKB (Polikarpov), Russia
Crew:	One
Maximum speed:	463 km/h (288 mph)
Weapons:	Four machine guns; up to 100 kg (220 lb) of bombs or two rockets

The Soviet fighter, Polikarpov I-16 had new features like retractable landing gears. It was successfully deployed during the Spanish Civil War and the Soviet-Japanese border war of 1939

The B-17 Flying Fortress was the first heavy bomber ever to be mass-produced. It was mainly used for daytime bombing of German factories during World War II

Retractable landing gear

Another significant change of this period was the introduction of the retractable landing gear. Earlier, aircraft had fixed wheels that could not be folded after take-off. This increased the drag or friction, slowing the aircraft down. With retractable or folding landing gear, the wheels were tucked into the fuselage when not in use.

The Messerschmitt Bf 109 was the first fighter to be made completely of metal and have enclosed cockpit and retractable landing gears

Messerschmitt Bf 109

Manufactured by:	Messerschmitt AG, Germany
Crew:	One
Maximum speed:	630 km/h (391 mph)
Weapons:	Two machine guns; two rockets; one cannon; upto 250 kg (550lb) bombs

B-17 Flying Fortress

Manufactured by:	Boeing IDS, U.S.A.
Crew:	Ten
Maximum speed:	462 km/h (287 mph)
Weapons:	13 machine guns; 4,364 kg (9,600 lb) bombs

Era of the bombers

Unlike fighter planes, bombers were not well developed during World War I. In the beginning, pilots just dropped bombs over the side of the cockpit. As the war progressed, heavier and more efficient aircraft were built solely for this purpose. After World War I the major countries focussed on developing bigger and faster bombers that would change the nature of warfare. Among the most successful aircraft of this period were the Junkers Ju 87 dive bomber and the Flying Fortress.

World War I Fighters

During World War II, German forces used the blitzkrieg tactic. Blitzkrieg, meaning 'lightening war', was the military tactic by which sudden attacks left the enemy stunned and unable to defend themselves. Their speed and size made fighters particularly successful at this kind of attack.

Messerschmitt Bf 110

Manufactured by:	Messerschmitt AG, Germany
Crew:	Three
Maximum speed:	600 km/h (373 mph)
Weapons:	Two cannons; five machine guns

The Luftwaffe fighters

In the early years of the war, the Luftwaffe (German air force) spread terror across the skies of Eastern and Western Europe with their superior combat aircraft. The Messerschmitt Bf 110, a twin-engine heavy fighter was the Luftwaffe's main night fighter. However, this efficient fighter-bomber proved almost worthless during daytime air raids during the Battle of Britain. Other Luftwaffe fighters included the Messerschmitt Me 262–the first jet-engined fighter–the Focke- Wulf Fw 190 and the Heinkel He 162.

The Messerschmitt Bf 110 did not have the manoeuvrability and speed required for a daylight fighter. However, its range and firepower made the aircraft a powerful night fighter

Battle of Britain

The extraordinary success enjoyed by the Germans in the beginning made the Luftwaffe overconfident. In 1940, the Royal Air Force of Britain went to war with a total of about 700 fighters, including 32 Hawker Hurricane squadrons and 19 Spitfire squadrons, against the much superior Luftwaffe comprising about 2,500 bombers and fighters! Despite this huge divide, the British air attack forced the Germans to call off the invasion. This marked a major turning point in the war.

OTHER EUROPEAN FIGHTERS

Other European nations did not have a huge array of combat aircraft, unlike Germany and Britain. However, aircraft like the French fighter Dewoitine D. 520, played a big role in the war. The Dewoitine D. 520 was a strong competitor to the Messerschmitt class of fighters due to its speed and manoeuvrability. Other Allied fighters were the Italian Macchi C. 202 and the Russian MiG-3 and Lavochkin La-5.

DEWOITINE D.520

Manufactured by:	Societe Nationale de Construction Aeronatiques du Midi (SNCAM), France
Crew:	Single
Maximum speed:	529 km/h (329 mph)
Weapons:	One cannon; four machine guns

The Dewoitine D.520 was the only French aircraft that came close to the German fighters. Unfortunately, very few Dewoitines were built during the war

SPITFIRE

Manufactured by:	Supermarine, U.K.
Crew:	Single
Maximum speed:	584 km/h (362 mph)
Weapons:	Eight machine guns

The Supermarine Spitfire along with Hawker Hurricane fighters were the stars of the Battle of Britain

European Bombers of WWII

During World War II, the countries involved realised that to defeat the enemy it was vital to strike at its industries, military bases and dams. Since such targets were often deep in enemy territory, only long-range bombers could carry out these tasks, making them the ultimate weapons of war.

Avro Lancaster

Manufactured by: Avro, U.K.
Crew: Seven
Maximum speed: 448 km/h (280 mph)
Weapons: Eight machine guns; up to 10,000 kg (22,000 lb) bombs

British bombers

Britain had some of the best bombers at its service, including the Avro Lancaster and de Havilland Mosquito. The most notable mission of the Lancaster was the bombing of the Ruhr Valley dams in North Rhine-Westphalia, Germany. The Mosquito was a light and speedy aircraft, useful as a day or night fighter. Other bombers included the sturdy but slow Wellington, with which Britain began the World War.

The Avro Lancaster was the main night bomber of the Royal Air Force. This bomber had a huge bay to carry bombs and the most advanced communication systems of the time

German bombers

The Junkers were the mainstay of the German bomber line-up. The Ju 88 was a medium range bomber that could carry a great deal of ammunition. It was also an excellent night fighter. The Heinkel 111, a medium range bomber, was also widely used until the end of the war. The Heinkel was especially effective during the first phase of the London Blitz. The Junkers 87 Stuka dive bombers, yet another favourite, was used extensively during the Battle of Britain.

Other bombers

The Petlyakov 2 was the best Russian bomber in the war. It was fast and agile. Russia's long-range bomber, the Ilyushin 4, was used to devastate Berlin, East Germany, and German-occupied territory in Eastern Europe and Russia. Another major bomber of the time was the Italian Savoya-Marchetti 79. This light bomber could carry a considerable amount of ammunition and was used mainly as a torpedo bomber.

The Stuka dive bombers had wind-powered sirens fixed to their wheels. These sirens wailed as wind struck them during dives, designed to scare the enemy. The wailing sirens earned the bombers the nickname, "Trumpets of Jericho"

Junkers Ju 87

Manufactured by:	Junkers Flugzeug und Motorenwerke AG, GErmany
Crew:	Two
Speed:	310 km/h (193 mph)
Weapons:	Three machine guns; one 250kg (551lb) bomb

The Attack on Pearl Harbor

At first, the United States decided to keep out of World War II. However, the Japanese were worried about the presence of the U.S. Navy in the Pacific. On December 7, 1941, the Japanese launched an air attack on the American fleet at Pearl Harbor to eliminate this danger.

Mighty carriers

Huge ships carrying combat aircraft had been introduced into the navies of all major countries following World War I. Aircraft carriers were, however, tested for the first time during the Pearl Harbor attack. Over 350 Japanese planes, in two groups, attacked the U.S. naval base. The first group mainly targeted the U.S. naval ships, while the second group bombed airfields on the island. By the end of the attack, the U.S. lost more than 2,400 men, almost all their combat aircraft and eight battleships.

Japanese bombers bombarding U.S. naval vessels and airstrip at the Pearl Harbor

Japanese Zeroes

The Japanese did not have a separate air force during the war. Instead, combat aircraft were an extended part of both the Japanese army and navy. The naval air service was stronger and well known for its Mitsubishi Zeroes, which played an important role in the Pearl Harbor attack. The Model 21 Zeroes were specially built for use on board aircraft carriers.

A6M2 Zero

Manufactured by: Mitsubishi, Japan
Type: single-seat fighter-bomber
Maximum speed: 540 km/h (336 mph)
Weapons: Two machine guns; two cannons: up to 60 kg (132 lb) bombs; two 250 kg (551 lb) kamikaze bombs

The Mitsubishi Zeroes were highly manoeuvrable and had great firepower

The bombers

The Zeroes were supported by the Aichi D3A dive-bombers, codenamed 'Val'. Later on, it was replaced by the more powerful Yokosuka D4Y Suisei. Special Japanese fighter units called Kamikaze, or Divine Wind, conducted suicide attacks on enemy ships. The Yokosuka D4Y Suisei and Nakajima Ki-115 were widely used for such attacks. During the war, about 2,800 Kamikaze attacks sunk 34 U.S. ships and damaged 368 others.

The Aichi D3A carrier-borne dive bomber played a major role in the Pearl Harbor attack. They were also used in kamikaze missions towards the end of the war

Aichi D3A

Manufactured by: Aichi Kokuki KK, Japan
Type: Two-seat dive bomber
Maximum speed: 386 km/h (240 mph)
Weapons: Three machine guns; two 60 kg (132 lb) bombs; one fixed 250 kg (551 lb) bomb

Enter the Americans

The devastation at Pearl Harbor greatly angered the Americans. The decision to stay out of the war was reversed. The U.S. declared war on Japan, and shortly afterwards on Germany. The course of World War II was greatly influenced by the superior planes developed by the U.S.

Curtiss P-40E

Manufactured by: Curtiss-Wright Corporation, U.S.A.
Type: Single seat fighter-bomber
Maximum speed: 583 km/h (362 mph)
Weapons: Six machine guns; 317 kg (700 lb) bombs

Early American fighters

The U.S. had a good collection of fighter aircraft even at the time of the Pearl Harbor attack. However, the Japanese strategy of surprise attacks on the U.S. air bases prevented them from responding quickly. The only resistance came from P-36 Hawks and P-40 Warhawks. The P-40 was used extensively by Allied forces across the world. It was sturdy and more efficient than most of its Japanese counterparts, but could not fly very high.

Over 13,700 P-40 fighters were produced during the war. They were used by 28 countries

The star fighters

Other major fighters used during the war were the Grumman F6F Hellcat and the Lockheed P-38 Lightning, both were more than a match for the light Japanese planes. The carrier-based Hellcat was in fact responsible for 75 per cent of all aerial victories by the U.S. in the Pacific Ocean. The other U.S. fighter to leave its mark on the war was the P-51 Mustang. The P-51 played a vital role in defeating the Luftwaffe and giving the Allied forces complete air superiority over Germany.

P-51 Mustang

Manufactured by: North American Aviation, U.S.A.
Type: Single-seat, bomber escort, fighter-bomber
Maximum speed: 704 km/h (437 mph)
Weapons: Six machine guns; up to 907 kg (2,000 lb) bombs; ten rockets

B-29 SUPERFORTRESS (*ENOLA GAY*)

Manufactured by:	Boeing IDS, U.S.A.
Type:	Ten crew, four-engine heavy bomber
Maximum speed:	587 km/h (365 mph)
Weapons:	12 machine guns; one cannon; 9,072 kg (20,000 lb) bombs

The B-29 Superfortress, named *Enola Gay*, became the first aircraft in history to drop an atomic bomb. The aircraft dropped the atomic bomb, *Little Boy* over Hiroshima on August 6, 1945

BOMBERS TO THE FORE

The American strategy in World War II was to rely heavily on its bombers. Initially, the unescorted bombers suffered huge losses due to enemy fire. Later, when the P-51 Mustang, the first long-range fighter, accompanied bombing squads fewer U.S. bombers were shot down. In the Pacific the U.S. Air Force used the B-29 Superfortress to launch attacks on Japan from China. The B-29 was also used to drop the first atomic bombs over the Japanese cities of Hiroshima and Nagasaki, in August 1945.

The P-51 Mustang was one of the most successful combat aircraft of World War II

Flying into the Jet Age

The first jet-powered combat aircraft was the German Messerschmitt Me 262 built during World War II. After the war, the British took the lead. Within a few years Britain had several jet fighters, two naval jets and even a jet-powered seaplane.

Initial lead

Britain was the only Allied power to have a jet fighter squadron before the end of the war. The Gloster Meteors of the Royal Air Force defended Britain from German V-1 bombs. Britain also introduced the single-engine de Havilland DH-100 Vampire in 1946. The Sea Vampire was the first jet aircraft to operate from an aircraft carrier. Apart from developing several other jet aircraft, the British also built a single seat jet seaplane called the "Squirt" which however, never took to air.

Gloster Meteor

Manufactured by:	Gloster Aircraft Company, U.K.
Crew:	One
Maximum speed:	668 km/h (415 mph)
Weapons:	Four cannons

The Gloster Meteor was only the second jet-powered fighter in history. It was extensively used during the Korean War in 1950

P-80 Shooting Stars were slowly replaced by the more effective F-86 Sabres as, the former were not advanced enough to face the much superior Russian aircraft

American efforts

The United States entered the jet age in 1942 with their Bell XP-59. However, this fighter was never used in combat. The first American jet fighter to see action was the Lockheed P-80 Shooting Star. This jet-powered combat aircraft was used extensively in the Korean War. The Republic F-84 was another first generation jet-powered fighter that served with distinction in the Korean War. However, the most successful combat aircraft of the jet age to serve in the Korean War was undoubtedly the F-86A Sabre.

P-80 Shooting Star

Manufactured by:	Lockheed Martin, USA
Crew:	One
Maximum speed:	966 km/h (601 mph)
Weapons:	Six machine guns; two 454 kg (1001 lb) bombs; 10-16 rockets

MESSERSCHMITT ME 262

Manufactured by:	Messerschmitt-Blkow-Blohm, Germany
Crew:	One
Maximum speed:	870 km/h (540 mph)
Weapons:	Four cannons; 454 kg (1000lb) bombs; 24 rockets

The jet-powered Messerschmitt Me 262 was not very successful during the war, but it was responsible for the subsequent revolution in aircraft design

RUSSIAN RESPONSE

Russia was quick to realise that it would need to enter the jet age to keep up with military technology. Four design teams took up the challenge to produce the first Russian jet combat aircraft. Two of them came up with prototypes within six months. On April 24, 1946, Artem Mikoyan and Mikhail Gurevich won the contest and their MiG-9 became the first Russian jet to fly. It was followed by the Yakovlev Yak-15.

The MiG-9 was mainly used in ground attacks as the aircraft design had many problems and its performance was poor

Supersonic Fighters

After the jet age, the next milestone was to get combat aircraft to fly faster than the speed of sound. Guided missiles were also first developed at this time. The early supersonic aircraft gave up agility and bomb carrying capacity in favour of speed and the ability to gain height rapidly.

The F-100 Super Sabre deployed in Vietnam was later replaced by F-4 and F-105 fighter-bombers

F-100 Super Sabre

Manufactured by:	North American Aviation, U.S.A.
Crew:	One
Maximum speed:	1,390 km/h (864 mph)
Weapons:	Four cannons; up to 3,190 kg (7,033 lb) of bombs; missiles and rockets

Breaking the sound barrier

The F-100 Super Sabre was the first U.S. fighter capable of supersonic speed. It broke the sound barrier on its first flight and set a speed record in October 1953 at 1,215 km/h (755.149 mph). The Super Sabre, especially its F-100D variant,

was widely used in the Vietnam War. The MiG-19 was the first Soviet combat aircraft to break the sound barrier. Production of MiG-19s first started in 1954, and some continue in service to this day. The English Electric Lightning of Britain is remembered for the fact that it held the world air-speed record for being over twice the speed of sound.

Improved designs

Achieving speeds faster than sound was just the first step towards a new generation of fighters. Aircraft designers had to improve performance and efficiency to cope with the challenges of the modern world. Swing-wings were developed to reduce friction and increase speed. This innovation helped the aircraft to sweep its wings back during high speeds and at the same time bring it back to the normal position in lower speeds.

New age controls

Increased speeds naturally led to the development of super light aircraft. Weapons were made lighter and lightweight metal alloys were used to build these fighters. Another significant change came with fly-by wire control systems. These systems use computers to control the aircraft, thereby getting rid of heavy cables. Modern fighters also have light and responsive controls, which make them more agile and easy to manoeuvre.

The Su-27 was one of the first aircraft to be built with using high amounts of titanium making the huge aircraft much lighter. It was also the first Soviet combat aircraft to have fly-by-wire controls

Sukhoi Su-27

Manufactured by: Sukhoi Design Bureau, Russia
Crew: One
Maximum speed: 2,494 km/h (1,550 mph)
Weapons: 1cannon; up to 6,000 kg (13,228 lb) of missiles and bombs

The F-14 Tomcat was one of the first fighters to have swing wings. The aircraft was agile and proved very effective as an interceptor

F-14 Tomcat

Manufactured by: Grumman Aerospace Corporation, U.S.A.
Crew: Two
Maximum speed: 2,485 km/h (1,544 mph)
Weapons: One cannon; air-to-air missiles; iron bombs

Supersonic Bombers

After supersonic fighters it was the turn of the bombers to break the sound barrier. The Convair B-58 Hustler was the world's first supersonic bomber, capable of flying over targets at Mach 2 (twice the speed of sound).

B-58 Hustler

The B-58 Hustler, of the U.S. Airforce, was a revolutionary bomber in more ways than one. One of its unique features was a tailless delta wing that helped the aircraft to reduce friction. The wing also enabled the aircraft to achieve high speeds even at low altitudes. The most amazing feature of the B-58 was its ejection capsule, which made it possible for the crew to eject out of the bomber even while travelling at twice the speed of sound. The normal ejection seats of that time did not have this ability.

B-58 Hustler

Manufactured by:	Consolidated Vultee Aircraft Corporation (Convair), U.S.A.
Crew:	Five
Maximum speed:	2,126 km/h (1,321 mph)
Weapons:	One cannon; up to 640kg (1,400 lb) of conventional and nuclear bombs

Despite its exceptional performance, the B-58 Hustler was retired by 1970 due to its high cost and maintenance

B-1 Lancer

Manufactured by:	Boeing IDS, U.S.A.
Crew:	Four
Maximum speed:	1,329 km/h (825.31 mph)
Weapons:	up to 34,000 kg (74,957 lb) of bombs

Other American bombers

The B-1 Lancer is the backbone of the long-range bomber force belonging to the U.S. Air Force. It has been used in several successful operations led by the U.S., including the ones in Iraq, Kosovo and Afghanistan. This bomber also has variable geometry wings, which means that the angle of its wings can be changed at different times while the aircraft is in flight.

The B-1 Lancer has been highly successful during Operation Enduring Freedom in Afghanistan and Operation Iraqi Freedom

Soviet bombers

The Tupolev Tu-22M also has wings, which can be swept back when it is flying faster than the speed of sound. The Soviets used the Tu-22M extensively in their war in Afghanistan for carpet bombing (dropping a shower of bombs). The Tu-22M is designed to carry conventional as well nuclear bombs. However, the Tupolev Tu-160 is perhaps the most successful supersonic bomber developed by the Soviet Union. This bomber resembles the American B-1 Lancer but is much larger and faster than the American bomber. It is also the heaviest combat aircraft ever built. The Tu-160 has swing-wings and fly-by-wire controls. This bomber replaced the Tu-22M and continues to be used by Russia and other former Soviet nations.

Tu-22M

Manufactured by:	Tupolev Design Bureau, Russia
Crew:	Four
Maximum speed:	2,160 km/h (1,350 mph)
Weapons:	One cannon; up to 24,000 kg (52,910 lb) of bombs

During the Cold War, the threat posed by the Tu-22M bomber was such that the U.S. government increased the country's defence budget to help build equally advanced bombers and fighters

Modern Combat Aircraft

The demands of modern warfare require strong, efficient, agile and up-to-date combat aircraft – all at low cost and low maintenance. The latest developments include glass cockpits, thrust vectoring, supercruise, stealth technology and use of lightweight materials like alloys, glass and plastic.

Sukhoi Su-30 MKI

Manufactured by: Corporation (Russia) and Hindustan Aeronautics Ltd (India)
Crew: Two
Maximum speed: 1,350 km/h (839 mph)
Weapons: One 30 mm cannon; 14 missiles

The Sukhoi Su-30 MKI is a highly manoeuvrable fighter with thrust vectoring

Supercruise

Supercruising aircraft can fly faster than the speed of sound without afterburners. Afterburners use up a lot of fuel and reduce flying time. The first aircraft to go supersonic in level flight, without afterburners, was the English Electric Lightning. All modern combat aircraft, like the Eurofighter Typhoon and the F-22 Raptor are supercruisers. Thrust vectoring technology endows modern fighters with amazing agility, allowing them to make 90 degree turns.

The Nighthawk is made of radar absorbing materials and paints, and also has a unique shape that makes it almost undetectable to radar.

Stealth

Lockheed's F-117 Nighthawk was the first combat aircraft to use stealth technology successfully in overcoming detection by radar. However, it can carry very little fuel and weapons, and also does not have a radar of its own. Efforts are on to counter these problems, especially since stealth combat aircraft are expected to play an important role in future conflicts.

F-117 Nighthawk

Manufactured by: Lockheed Aeronautical Systems Co, U.S.A.
Crew: One
Maximum speed: 1,127 km/h (700 mph)
Weapons: up to 2,268 kg (5,000 lb) of bombs or missiles

Glass cockpits

Early aircraft cockpits were often crammed with dozens of dials and gauges that needed to be constantly monitored. Glass cockpits have just a few computer controlled displays of all the information that the pilot needs. In the F-15A Eagle, all important information is projected on the screen in front of the pilot. This enables the pilot to track down and shoot enemy aircraft without taking his eyes off it.

The F-15 Eagle was one of the first aircraft to have a Head-Up display system that projected flight information on a screen in front of the pilot

F-15A Eagle

Manufactured by:	Boeing (formerly McDonnell-Douglas), U.S.A.
Crew:	One
Speed:	2,575 km/h (1,600 mph)
Weapons:	One cannon; eight missiles; up to 7,300 kg (16094 lb) of bombs

Naval Combat Aircraft

Naval aviation began in 1912, when, for the first time, an aircraft took off from the British warship, HMS *Hibernia*. Today, naval aviation stands shoulder to shoulder with its air force counterpart.

The picture shows a combat aircraft getting ready for take off from the deck of a carrier

Carrier-based aircraft

Aircraft carriers are very large, but even so it is not easy to take off or land a plane on a ship, especially if it is moving. Carrier-based combat aircraft are usually small, with foldable wings, as there is a lack of space on carriers. They take off in the direction the ship is sailing and land from the rear. Some carriers have a steam-powered catapult that pushes the aircraft forward with force, allowing it to take off quickly. All aircraft that take off and land by taxiing have a tail hook attached to their tail. The tail hook is a claw-like device that grabs the thick arrestor wires stretched across the ship's deck as the aircraft lands, forcing the aircraft to halt.

Modern carrier aircraft

VTOL, or Vertical Take off and Landing reduces the risk of taking off or landing on ships. With VTOL, combat aircraft can lift up without taxiing, much like a helicopter. Aircraft are able to do this using the thrust vector technology, which enables the aircraft to direct the thrust from the main engines in any direction.

Yak-38

Manufactured by:	Yakovlev Design Bureau, Russia
Crew:	One
Maximum speed:	1050 km/hour (652mph)
Weapons:	One cannon, 1,000 kg (2,200 lb) of bombs

The Yakovlev Yak-38 was the Soviet Union's only VTOL combat aircraft. This aircraft could be guided by computer systems to land on the deck of the carrier without any help from the pilot

Ski-jump ramps

The biggest drawback of Vertical Take Off and Landing aircraft is that they cannot carry a great deal of weight. This is very important, as combat aircraft need to carry enough fuel and weapons for long-range operations. Ski jump runways provide the perfect solution for this problem. In this case, combat aircraft can take off normally, without catapults, as these short runways provide the necessary power. Moreover, in such instances, the aircraft can land vertically and avoid the use of arrestor wires.

AV-8B Harrier II

Manufactured by:	McDonnell Douglas, U.S.A.
Crew:	One
Maximum speed:	1000 km/h (629 mph)
Weapons:	One cannon; up to 5,987 kg (13,200 lb) of bombs and missiles

The AV-8B Harrier II is a V/STOL, or Vertical/Short Take-off and Landing, aircraft. It usually takes off from a carrier vertically, but is also capable of taking off with the help of a ski jump when the load is too heavy for a vertical take-off

Helicopters in Combat

Helicopters were first used for military purposes soon after they were invented in the early 1900s. The U.S. Army Air Corps asked Igor Sikorsky, a helicopter manufacturer, to develop a model for them.

XR-4

Type:	Two-seat, training and rescue
Manufactured by:	Sikorsky Aircraft Corporation, USA
Speed:	131 km/h (81 mph)
Maximum weight at take-off:	1,150 kg (2,535 lb)

In 1942, Sikorsky developed the XR-4 for the U.S. military. It was the world's first mass produced helicopter and also the first to use a single rotor

The Black Hawk has featured in many blockbuster films including *Clear and Present Danger* and *Black Hawk Down*

Attack helicopters

Attack helicopters are used in much the same way as attack aircraft are. These helicopters support troops on the ground by targeting enemy troops and tanks. Some helicopters like the Black Hawk often carry air-to-air missiles to attack enemy helicopters or aircraft. Naval attack helicopters, like the Sea Hawk, can be used to target enemy ships and even detect and destroy submarines.

Troop carriers

Helicopters are often used to transport troops to and from battlefields. Some like the CH-47 Chinook or the Mi-6 'Hook' can carry dozens of fully equipped troops. They can also be used to quickly airlift injured troops to the nearest hospital.

Mil Mi-6 Hook

Type:	Five-seat heavy transport helicopter
Manufactured by:	Mil Moscow Helicopter Plant, Russia
Crew:	Five
Maximum speed:	300 km/h (186 mph)
Maximum weight at take off:	41,700 kg (91,933 lb)

The Mi-6 was used for both military and civilian purposes. It could carry about 60 troops, or up to 12,000 kg of load. The Mi-6 continues to be used in some countries including China, Russia and Egypt

Sky crane helicopters

From their earliest days, helicopters have been used to lift men, weapons and machinery into the heart of the war zone. Helicopters like the CH-54 'Skycrane' or the Mi-10 'Harke'-B have little by way of a body, apart from the cockpit, the engine and the rotors, but their engines are powerful enough to lift several tonnes at a time. The CH-54 was often used in the Vietnam War to lift as many as 100 troops.

The CH-54 could also lift portable hospitals or tanks. Such helicopters were also used to retrieve aircraft that had been shot down

CH-54

Type:	Three-seat heavy-lift crane
Manufactured by:	Sikorsky Aircraft Corporation, U.S.A.
Maximum speed:	370 km/h (230 mph)
Maximum weight at take off:	21,319 kg (47,000 lb)

American Combat Helicopters

The United States has pioneered the development of helicopters for both civilian and military uses. Most of the major helicopter manufacturers, like Sikorsky, Bell and Boeing, are American. Helicopters have been a major part of the U.S. Army, Air Force, Navy and Marines ever since World War II.

Heavy duty helicopters

Large helicopters in the United States military, like the CH-53E Super Stallion, can lift nearly 17 tonnes of cargo. This enables them to lift armoured vehicles along with their crew! They are also helpful in retrieving downed aircraft. In fact, the Super Stallion, which is used by the U.S. Navy and Marines, can retrieve almost any aircraft.

The two rotors of the CH-47 Chinook give the helicopter extra power to lift loads as heavy as a tank

CH-47 Chinook

Manufactured by:	Boeing IDS, U.S.A.
Crew:	Three
Maximum speed:	296 km/h (184 mph)
Weapons:	None
Capacity:	30 troops

Helicopters in combat

The attack helicopters of the United States come armed with a variety of weapons. A top-of-the-line ground attack helicopter like Boeing's AH-64 Apache can fight a battalion of tanks with its 16 anti-tank missiles and 76 rockets. It can target ground troops with rapid-fire bursts from its 30 mm chain gun. However, despite its power, a helicopter can never match the speed of a fighter or the range of a bomber.

The AH-64 Apache is the main combat helicopter of the U.S. Army. It has seen combat in many conflicts including the Gulf War, Operation Enduring Freedom in Afghanistan and Operation Iraqi Freedom

Various models of the Sea Hawk have been developed for specific roles from troop transport and search and rescue missions, to anti-submarine warfare and ground attacks

SH-60 Sea Hawk

Manufactured by:	Sikorsky Aircraft Corporation, U.S.A.
Crew:	Three
Maximum speed:	233 km/h (145 mph)
Weapons:	One machine gun; two torpedoes

AH-64 Apache

Manufactured by:	Boeing IDS, U.S.A.
Type:	Two-seat attack helicopter
Maximum speed:	449 km/hour (279 mph)
Weapons:	One cannon; missiles and rockets

Helicopters in the U.S. Navy

The ease with which helicopters can take off and land from warships of all kinds gives them an edge over fixed wing combat aircraft. Apart from the usual roles of transporting troops, naval helicopters also have other uses. Some helicopters like the Sea Hawk or the Sea Knight are also used in search and rescue operations and in anti-submarine warfare. These helicopters have very sophisticated radar systems that enable them to detect objects under water, which they can then target and destroy using depth charges and torpedoes. Some are used to drop supplies, transport weapons and carry out medical evacuation.

European Combat Helicopters

The helicopter manufacturing industry in Europe has grown rapidly. In fact, today, the largest and the fastest combat helicopters are made outside the U.S. The Aerospatiale in France and the British Westland are some of the world's leading combat helicopter manufacturers.

Mil Mi-24 Hind

Manufactured by:	Mil Moscow Helicopter Plant, Russia
Crew:	Two
Maximum speed:	335 km/h (208 mph)
Weapons:	One cannon; up to 2,400 kg (5,291 lb) of bombs, missiles and rockets

Even the rotor blades of the Mi-24 are made of titanium to endure cannon fire

Russian helicopters

The Mil Helicopter Design Bureau's Mi-26 'Halo' is the largest combat helicopter in the world. It weighs 28 tonnes when empty and can lift 28 tonnes of cargo. It has two turboshaft engines that give the aircraft powerful lift. The Mil Moscow Helicopter Plant also makes one of the fastest combat helicopters, the Mi-24 'Hind'. This gunship has a heavily armoured body to withstand enemy fire.

British helicopters

The Westland Lynx is Britain's top attack helicopter. It is used in both the Army Air Corps and the Royal Navy's Fleet Air Arm. Westland's Sea King and its Commando variant have the longest range amongst all combat helicopters outside the United States. The Sea King is used by the Royal Navy for anti-submarine warfare and as an airborne early warning system.

French helicopters

The French anti-tank attack helicopter SA 341 Gazelle is one of the fastest combat helicopters in the world. Its speed results from its light weight. The Gazelle is also used for a variety of other operations including directing ground attack aircraft, medical evacuation, directing artillery fire and communications. Another popularly used French helicopter is the Aérospatiale Super Frelon. This helicopter has the longest range in the French military. It can fly up to 1,000 kilometres. The Super Frelon's sturdy build and long range makes it useful as a heavy-duty transport helicopter. Anti-submarine and anti-ship variants of the Super Frelon were also produced.

The Lynx was initially developed as a utility helicopter for both civilian and naval purposes. It was later modified as an attack helicopter for the army and the navy

Sea King

Manufactured by:	Westland Helicopters, U.K.
Crew:	Two to Four
Maximum speed:	232 km/h (144 mph)
Weapons:	Four depth charges or torpedoes

SA 341 Gazelle

Manufactured by:	Aerospatiale (France) and Westland Aircraft (U.K.) joint venture
Crew:	One or two
Maximum speed:	311 km/hour (193 mph)
Weapons:	Up to two machine guns or one cannon; missiles or rockets

The Gazelle is one of the fastest helicopters ever. It has seen service in all branches of the British armed forces as an attack helicopter, trainer and transport helicopter

Unmanned Combat Air Vehicles

Combat aircraft without a human pilot, are fast becoming a reality. Several countries are exploring the possibilities of unmanned combat air vehicles. Aircraft like the F/A-22 Raptor and the Eurofighter Typhoon will probably be the last fighters with a human pilot in the cockpit.

From reconnaissance to combat

The first unmanned combat vehicles (UCAVs) to be tested successfully by the military were reconnaissance aircraft. In the 1970s the idea was tested for use in fighters and bombers too. The U.S. Air Force launched the project 'HAVE LEMON' to develop UCAVs that could destroy enemy anti-aircraft guns and surface-to-air missiles on the ground. The project was successful in creating worldwide interest in aerial combat.

Current UCAV projects

By 1979, the HAVE LEMON project was shelved and the concept of the UCAV was forgotten for a while. However, the rapid progress in communication systems in recent years has once again revived UCAV experiments. One of the most popular projects is the Joint-UCAS, a collaborative effort by the U.S. Navy and Air Force to produce the Boeing X-45 and the Northrop Grumman X-47 Pegasus. Both have the ability to carry out ground attacks and perform defensive aerial combat.

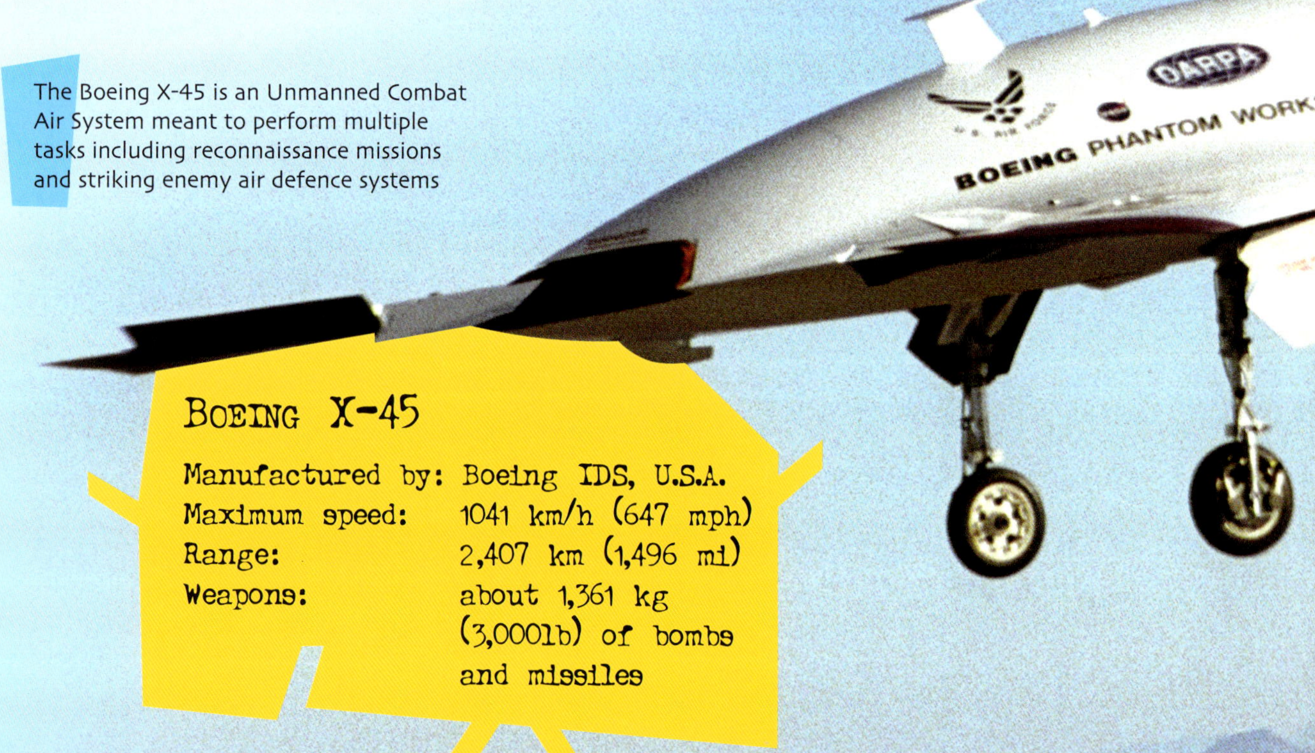

The Boeing X-45 is an Unmanned Combat Air System meant to perform multiple tasks including reconnaissance missions and striking enemy air defence systems

Boeing X-45

Manufactured by:	Boeing IDS, U.S.A.
Maximum speed:	1041 km/h (647 mph)
Range:	2,407 km (1,496 mi)
Weapons:	about 1,361 kg (3,000lb) of bombs and missiles

RQ-1 Predator

Manufactured by:	General Atomics Aeronautical Systems, U.S.A.
Maximum speed:	217km/h (135mph)
Range:	731 km (454mi)
Weapons:	over 2,000 kg (907 lb) of bombs and missiles

The RQ-1 Predator, an Unmanned Aerial Vehicle, has successfully been used in combat and many secret operations by the CIA

Advantage UCAV

UCAVs have a number of benefits. They are cheaper, require less maintenance and do not need human pilots. Operating costs for a UCAV would also be very low as operators can be trained through simulations, thereby avoiding loss of aircraft and lives during training. UCAVs would also be able to dodge enemy missiles better as they can perform manoeuvres that are impossible for a manned combat aircraft. More importantly, UCAVs would be able to perform highly dangerous missions that could otherwise cost the lives of trained pilots. UCAVs could also be smaller and stealthier than manned aircraft. That is why countries apart from the U.S., like France, Sweden, South Africa and Israel, are also working on UCAV programmes.

Nightowl, an unmanned air vehicle belonging to the U.S. Marine Corps was used extensively for spying on enemy territories during Operation Iraqi Freedom in 2004-06

Combat Aircraft of the Future

The future belongs to multi-role combat aircraft, with all the features of present fighters and more. Some new generation aircraft with extraordinary agility and dogfight abilities include the F-22 Raptor, Joint Strike Fighter, Rafale and Eurofighter Typhoon.

Face of the Future

The F-22 Raptor, of the U.S. Air Force, is the face of future combat aircraft. This fighter has it all – stealth technology, computerised control systems, high manoeuvrability, supercruise and thrust vectoring. However, its most outstanding feature is its unique radar that can track several targets even in the worst weather conditions, while confusing enemy sensors at the same time. This makes the F-22 Raptor a powerful fighter.

F-22 Raptor

Manufactured by:	Lockheed Martin Aeronautics and Boeing IDS, U.S.A.
Crew:	Single
Maximum speed:	2,450 km/h (1,522 mph)
Weapons:	One gun; 10,550kg (23,259 lb) of bombs

The F-22 Raptor is considered to be more cost effective than other stealth aircraft like the F-117 Nighthawk and the B-2 Spirit

Joint Strike Fighter

The F-35 Joint Strike Fighter (JSF) is currently being developed jointly by the United States, Britain and many other partner countries. The Joint Strike Fighter will not only be used for tactical bombing but also for air-to-air combat. It is being designed on the same lines as the highly successful F-22 Raptor, only with better thrust vectoring capabilities.

Eurofighter Typhoon F2

Manufactured by:	BAE Systems, U.K.
Crew:	One or two
Maximum speed:	2,125 km/h (1,321 mph)
Weapons:	One cannon; up to 6,500 kg (14,330 lb) of bombs and missiles

European effort

The most well known European combat aircraft projects are the Eurofighter and Rafale. Following the current trend of multi-role strike fighters, Britain, Germany, Italy and Spain jointly developed the Eurofighter Tyhoon. This fighter combines agility, stealth technology and performance, making it the best fighter aircraft; second only to the F-22 Raptor. The Rafale, belonging to the French Air Force and Navy, has also been developed as a multi-role fighter and has all the features of the Typhoon and F-22 Raptor.

The Eurofighter Typhoon is said to be as efficient and agile as the F-22 Raptor

The Joint Strike Fighter is expected to be more advanced than both the Eurofighter and the F-22 Raptor

F-35 Joint Strike Fighter

Manufactured by:	Joint venture by Lockheed Martin Aeronautics and Northrop Grumman, U.S.A. and BAE Systems, U.K.
Crew:	Single
Maximum speed:	2,250 km/h (1,398 mph)
Weapons:	One cannon; bombs and missiles

Glossary

Aerial – of or in the air

Afterburners – an additional part in a jet aircraft that gives extra thrust during take-off or supersonic flight

Agile – quick; lively; nimble

Air superiority – the dominance of the air force of one country over the enemy during a war

Ammunition dumps – a military facility that stores weapons and explosives

Aviation – of, or relating to aircraft

Conventional – traditional; usual

Depth charges – an anti-submarine weapon comprising a cylinder filled with explosives. A fuse is connected to the explosives, which can be set to go off at a specific depth. Depth charges are dropped into the water to destroy submerged submarines

Distinction - outstanding

Fixed wing aircraft – an aeroplane; any heavier-than-air craft that does not use its wings to generate power for flying

Fuselage – the main body of an aircraft that carries the crew and passengers or cargo

Grenade – a small bomb with a fuse that is usually thrown by hand or discharged from a rifle or a launcher

Guided missile – a missile that can seek out and follow its target

Innovative – creative; novel

Interrupter gear – a device in a machine gun mounted on a combat aircraft that prevents the gun from firing when the propeller or any other part of the aircraft is in the gun's way. This allows for the firing of the aircraft through the spinning propellers without the bullet striking the blades

Mainstay – basis; primary support

Manoeuvre – an action or move made for a gain

Milestone – an important moment or event

Obsolete – outdated; out of fashion

Propeller – a device consisting of blades attached to a shaft, the spinning of which propels a boat or an aircraft forward

Reconnaissance – investigation survey

Retractable – something that can be retracted or withdrawn; foldable

Retrieve - recover

Rotor – the rotating part of an aircraft, as in the rotor of a helicopter

Simulation – a training programme or a real world event that is imitated by a computer programme

Sound barrier – the sudden increase in drag (air resistance) that an aircraft nearing supersonic speed experiences

Squadron – an air-force unit made up of three or four flights consisting of 12-24 aircraft

Supercruiser – aircraft that can cruise at supersonic speeds without the help of afterburners

Surveillance - observation

Thrust vectoring – the ability of an aircraft to direct the thrust from its main engines either downwards or upwards

Unescorted - unaccompanied

Index